MAGIC, MYSTERY AND WONDER

Swapna Khandeparkar

INDIA • SINGAPORE • MALAYSIA

ISBN
Paperback 979-8-89632-724-0
Hardcase 979-8-89632-822-3

Index

Authors Note 7

Authors' Introduction 9

1. A Concoction Called Love 11
2. In That Moment, I Existed No More 13
3. Breakthroughs 15
4. Love and Hate 17
5. I Am Whole 18
6. Life and Death 20
7. If You Have a Dream, You Got to Protect It! 22
8. The Happiest Moment of My Life 24
9. I Understand 26
10. Restart 29
11. The Voice Inside 31
12. I Let You Go 33
13. Love and Loss 37
14. Only the Truth Will Set You Free! 40
15. The Home That Speaks Love and Peace to Me 45
16. The Pregnant Pause 49
17. Illusion v/s Reality 52

18. The Pedestal 56
19. A Soul Shock Towards Ascension 60
20. The Daily Practice 65
21. Life Through a New Lens 69
22. Depths of Love 73
23. A Shift in Perspective 76
24. Soham 79
25. Many Lives Many Masters 83
26. Galaxies and Their Pathways 87
27. Loveful Chaos 89
28. Touch 93
29. Deep Incisions 96
30. Unrequited Love 98
31. Rest 101
32. Love Expressions 102
33. Void 104
34. Transition 107
35. Love Letter to My Body 110
36. There Is Only One You 114
37. What Makes You Special? 116
38. What Does Fun Mean to Me? 118
39. Let Me 121
40. Gifted 123
41. The Gift of Life 124

42. Finding Happiness in Everyday Life 126
43. Closure 127
44. Muse 129
45. Vent 130
46. Art 133
47. What It Is to Be a Woman 134
48. Life Through a New Lens: (2.0) 136
49. An Embodiment of Love 141
50. Emotions in Motion 144

Authors Note

Welcome to my second collection of poetry, where I invite you to embark on a journey of self-discovery, love and transformation. These poems are a reflection of my own soul's journey, distilled from moments of joy, heartache and growth.

Within these pages, I share my inner most thoughts, emotions and experiences, hoping to resonate with your own soul song. May you find solace, inspiration, and connection in these words and may they guide you deeper into the beauty and complexity of your own soul.

The collection represents a progression of my poetic voice, exploring new themes, styles while maintaining the authenticity and vulnerability that defines my work. I am grateful for the opportunity to share my art with you and I hope these poems will become a cherished companion on your own journey of self-discovery.

I dedicate this book to my mentor, Ms. Megha Bajaj for bringing out the magic through my writings,my gurus and teachers who have been instrumental in my healing journey, Yogacharya Ms. Sandhya Dixit and Shri Santosh Pandey, from Kaivalyadham, Lonavala. My parents Shri D C Kunder and Mrs Sharayu Kunder, for supporting me wholeheartedly throughout my life, especially through the dark phases of my life. My friend Ms. Nikita Rajput for being the pathfinder through my writing journey, healing work and reviving my interests in the long lost passions in art.

I am grateful to have met them in this beautiful journey of life and the experiences I have been through.

Thankyou for embracing my words, and I look forward to connecting with you through the universal language of poetry. Thankyou is a very short word for everything summed up in this book. Love and Light.

Authors' Introduction

Welcome to my collection of poems, where I invite you to join me on a journey of self-discovery, love and transformation. As a writer, I have always been fascinated by the power of words to capture the human experience and connect us across time and space.

Through my poetry I aim to create a sense of resonance and community where readers can find solace, inspiration and connection. I believe that words have the power to heal, to uplift and to transform us, and I hope that these poems will be a source of comfort, guidance and joy for you.

So come, join me on this journey into world of words and let us explore the depths of human heart together.

A Concoction Called Love

I hope you find 'Love', someday,
A roar that flexes your throbbing heart
A tune which entwines magically with your breath,
An emotion that feels like you've arrived home.

Nevertheless, do not to confine love to a person,
It's a fiery territory to tread of heartache and limerence,
Because just as the rivers and the seas,
Love is meant only to flow.

Love encapsulates as wind in the mountains,
As peace in prayers, as blessings of a mother,
As rains in the parched lands of an exclusive summer,
Evolved are those who know how to surrender to love.

You may blame it for not overstaying,
But do not restrict its flow, when it has served its purpose.
It may present you as a Loss, when it leaves you for good,
Only to be manifested where it is sought the most.

There is always surrender in the not knowing,
Why love fails to stay for the most of us,
I know not enough, but I know for sure it presents itself,
When we least expect it to show up in our lives.

Somehow Love is wiser than we think, it is,
It will catch you at your worst, and will leave you at your best,
The only courage we can summon is Peace
which will grace itself as the harbinger of Love.

In That Moment, I Existed No More

What is important to you?
It whispers to her in uncanny ways,
After all the ways of endlessly seeking,
What is it that gives you peace?

She delves upon these questions, like an afterthought,
The sound of "OM" simply purges her soul,
Yet there are moments when,
The pull to seek remains undefined.

The soul talks to her in myriad ways,
Through her dreams and angel numbers
and she just knows,
She is divinely guided to walk the path.

Like the piano notes that calm her chaos,
Alike the bright colours that kiss the forlorn pale canvases,
The fragrance of mud that lingers long after the showers,
Her soul wants to sing a song of Love.

She seeks a companion, for long time now,
A confidant that makes her feel loved,
In cascading moments of her vulnerabilities,
Parched enough to belong to"the One".

She stays, betrays herself enough,
Nevertheless, with the fabrication in her youth,
To seek it in the external realms,
Unaware of the ways of the manipulative world.

Until her soul thwarts her efforts to seek Love,
Like a mother protecting her child,
She grieves until she feels better again,
The soul absolves itself from the heaviness.

She sits peacefully in her sanctuary,
The light, heals her from the enmeshed dualities,
Until her nervous system feels safe again,
Seeking the only altar within, her Heart!

Tears cleanse the pathways on her journey, inwards.
She finds her 'Home' ultimately with a realisation that,
It was always 'HIM' she was forever seeking,
And in that insanely surreal moment, she exists "No More"!!

Breakthroughs

The Universe rewards us,
With things we are capable of receiving,
Only if we understand how magically,
Our mind works.

The wiring of our brain
Is interconnected with the patterns
That make their essence known
In the whirlpool of thoughts.

Once we begin to understand
The essence of our own thought
It becomes easier to look at it
In a conscious way.

Rather than behaving in ways
Of Programmed patterns of behaviour.
We begin to look at it and replace it
With a new thought that rewires our brains.

The neurological pathways
When they begin to accept new information
Need to discard the old thought
And simply accept the new ones reinstated.

Once the body is attuned to itself
And welcomes a new thought
In its own discerning ways,
It experiences the change first hand.

Which in turn unknowingly,
Instructs the mind to be in sync,
With the body,
For harmonious union with the thoughts.

The evolved patterns of thought
Build layer upon layer ensure
New pathways for the mind
To take a leap of faith in the unknown.

To bring in new experiences
And new spaces to evolve in ways
Not known earlier and to create
Fresh breakthroughs in our lives.

Love and Hate

The absence of Love is indifference.
How does one know that he is not loved enough?

If we observe creatures around us closely
Love demands its essence in uncanny ways,

A creature in pain, and tears over something
Is simply seeking to be embraced in a hug,

Until he let goes of the barriers within,
For love to be bestowed upon him.

The energy exchange with hate is million times more than Love,
Yet Love is powerful than any other emotions, because

Love is a high vibrant frequency which leads us
To Simplicity and the Divine Himself.

I Am Whole

I am not the body
I am not the mind,
I am not the thought, that fails to impress,
I am radiant energy—hence I am whole.

I am not the successes
I am not the failures either,
Nor the material things aplomb
I am eternal abundance –hence I am whole.

I don't identify myself
With the ambitions or success
I am not the ecstasy or remorse either,
I am eternal bliss-hence I am whole.

I am not the relationships
I am not the roles you identify with,
I am not the theories played by the mind,
I am the masterpiece of God himself—hence I am whole.

I am not the pain,
I am not the joys you experience,
I am not the love you seek outside,
I am love itself—hence I am whole.

I am not a sojourn to celebrate,
I am not someone who fears the death,
I am a part of His divine light,
I am an eternal soul—hence I am whole.

Life and Death

Where do you go to from here?
From where have you been?
Do you remember who you are?
Since how long have you been?

Is this a play of birth and rebirth?
Or a lesson to be learnt on Earth?
Let your soul burn by these questions,
Then you may seek profound answers.

You don't have a clue yet,
Your breath holds the clues to the mysteries,
You tend to seek within and without,
Which is your forever guiding light.

Hold on, to it!
Until it flickers away,
When will you respect the force within?
Bestowed upon you as a gift!

Learn the basics from the beginning,
So that the end becomes a fairy tale,
Don't wallow in self-pity,
When you were given a fair chance.

Come home to yourself,
Whilst still there is time for you,
Make peace with grief,
And everything that sanctifies you.

Love your life deeply,
As tomorrow is never guaranteed,
Leave the tapestry of reincarnation,
You have played enough, Dear soul!

If You Have a Dream, You Got to Protect It!

Don't let anyone tell you, you can't do it.
If you have a dream, you got to protect it.

Don't ever let the fire inside you die.
If it is a soul calling, you can never escape it.

Don't let fear distract you from your path,
Understand that its work is, to defy you.

Don't let circumstances make you feeble,
They can change even when things look pale.

Don't fear failure,
Because you learn only to rise.

Don't fear being alone in adversity,
The Sun is alone, yet shines bright every day.

Don't let the people, determine your why,
Because only God knows how to shape up your Now.

Don't ever lose your faith in God,
Because He will be beside you, always!

The Happiest Moment of My Life

A yearning to connect with a soul
Who would simply understand me,
A refuge, from the worldly chaos,
My heart simply sought a Home.

Since my prayers were as
fluent as my breathe,
I met a soul, who simply felt like
The missing piece of the puzzle.

I refused to believe what the connection was,
But it was only in a brief
distancing from him
Was I showed the signs by the Divine,

He felt like my own split soul
Someone who just gets me at all times.
A mentor,
whenever the situations called for.

An assignment of shadow work
gifted by God,
A solstice that knows not the beginning,
but has an inkling of the end.

I am happy, I have met him,
I pray to God to bless me with
The wisdom to honour His gift,
I believe in a harmonious union with him.

He reminded me of who I was,
and where I have come from,
To pursue my soul calling,
With him being my mentor by my side.

I am grateful to God- I met him
Not only to realise, what remains oblivious to me
But also to understand what unconditional love truly is,
A blessing which I will forever cherish- with love!

I Understand

I understand what repression feels like,
To not be allowed to express oneself,
I understand what being stifled feels like,
defined by false notions of society.

I understand not feeling heard feels like,
Hence I vow not to repress my child's pain,
I don't shove her voice,
I encourage her to be real with it.

I understand what it feels like growing up
In a dysfunctional family,
I relate well to the out-casts,
and the rebels.

I understand why people choose
not to be in a relationship,
Beyond their marriage-able age,
I understand they have different choices from life.

I now understand how bringing up a child,
Is a huge responsibility for the adults,
But what I understand is,
the parents need to be happy.

I understand how a broken heart
Does not allow you to sleep peacefully,
But I also understand that,
It is only my responsibility to protect my heart.

I understand how the soul feels
When it roams without a purpose,
Without learning its lessons,
I now understand what it needs to seek liberation.

I understand how things can go haywire,
Inspite of doing everything it takes,
But now I also understand that,
God always has a bigger plan.

I understand that I am unable to manifest
From the space of lack,
I can manifest anything,
only if I continue to raise my vibrations.

I understand that pain is a part of our growth
But what I also now understand that,
We don't need to focus on pain,
When we are the master creators of our life.

I understand how easy it is to quit after trying,
But now I also understand the importance
Of knowing when to quit gracefully,
When time demands our ascension to the next level!

Restart

When the Sun sets, and the land is dark
The night is restart towards a new dawn.

When hope fails to raise the spirit,
Only action restarts the courage within you.

When things go wrong as they sometimes will,
Every morning is a fresh restart to your story.

When adverse situations blur your vision,
courage will make sense to restart anew.

When you blame God for dismantled dreams
He will gift you a blessing to restart your hope.

When you fail to believe in yourself
there is no one coming to restart life for you.

When you strive relentlessly to fulfil your dreams,
God ensures that you win, in the game of life.

When you find, everything is collapsing around you,

Know that faith in God holds the restart mode in your life.

The Voice Inside

A silent dialogue of your soul
That embosses its presence in your mind
You will need to listen to,
no matter what,

It will keep ringing in your ears,
Until you pay real attention to it,
Respect its yearning to be heard,
At some point you have to listen.

Make space for the thought to be placed
In the sanctuary of your heart
Gently acknowledging
and allowing it space.

The voice won't need your expression
if you allow it to flow free,
It will just need you to sit still,
your being shall allow it to float.

Don't deny its existence,
Acknowledge it as your
soul expression,
Something you would comprehend in time.

Pay enough attention to it,
Because it might be just that,
The voice of the Divine
trying to reach you in a state of stillness!

I Let You Go

When you're unsure which path to choose,
It is better to let things be,
Because whatever path you take,
It will lead you to letting go.

The clinging to something
Will not aid to your path towards Him,
The object of your attention,
Was never the final destination.

You may wonder why to let it go
When it means so much to you,
But God has his ways worked out for you,
Only if you let it go.

In releasing the attachment to the other
You are doing a favour to yourself,
Freeing him from the clutches
you hold so tight.

Everything that leads you to His Oneness,
Was only an instrument placed on your path,
So that you pay heed to what is important,
The situation, was a torch bearer for you.

Why would you hold on?
Is it because of your insecurities?,
You fail to see, dear child,
It is the divine plan, trying to teach you.

Everyone that leads to His path,
Should be honoured
Instead of being condemned for
Leaving you mid-way.

Why did you make the other
An object of your destination?
When the Ultimate goal
lies clearly ahead of you?

It will hurt, for some time,
Because your soul feels ripped off,
The co-dependent patterns
have been acting on you.

The pain was not deliberate,
it was not given to you by Him,
It is your own making,
the void that makes you cling.

To everything that makes you feel belonged,
But do you know how pained God feels,
when you detach from Him?
You were once whole—in oneness with Him.

When you were separated
from your mother's womb,
You have been seeking
the Oneness which you have lost,

Grieve as much as you want to,
until you reach a realisation,
That God has always been with you,
So do the angels and ascended masters,

Let go and let God,
If you tend to lose faith in Him,
He will give you what you desire,
but will it serve you?

you will come to a realisation,
That your ultimate goal was
to walk your path alone,
The other can be a torchbearer for you,,

The road to Him, may not be rosy,
But don't fear treading it alone,
realise only letting go
will bring you peace.

So that you become
a torch bearer for someone else,
Who needs you as a mentor
to take his journey towards Him! Amen!

Love and Loss

When you find love
And simply try hard to keep it,
It leaves you anxious
Wondering if it was real?

What you don't understand is,
The anxious attachment theory
You grew up with since childhood
Made you attached and clingy.

You would like to think,
That it is was real Love
But it was your abandonment wounds
Shining forth on you.

You may not trust the other,
But you haven't understood love
You believe that your co-dependency
Was your way of believing in attachment.

You have to look within to understand
Why Love has not chosen you yet,
Where are you going wrong with it,
When you were not choosing yourself.

When love doesn't overstay
Or chooses some time apart from you,
You may wonder
whether it is a Loss.

Love doesn't betray you,
Love only tests you and
it appears as a loss,
To ensure you learn self-love.

Love is noble, it is gentle,
It is only man who doesn't know
How to honour it when it is served
Because of his incapacity to receive it.

Love is divine,
it is all encompassing
It will lead you to growth,
Only if you believe.

Don't fall, rise in Love,
Because love knows only to Ascend,
In all dimensions of time and space,
And encompasses all beings on the planet.

Don't mistrust in love,
Because it is the only slivery light sword
Gifted from the heavens above, to see
Whether you stand its tests!

But if you fail in the tests,
You not only fail God
but your own soul
judging it before experiencing it fully.

Love is Divine,
And it is only meant to heal you
In ways you can't comprehend
Because God wants you to win, with Love!

Only the Truth Will Set You Free!

You will come on this planet,
Not knowing your mission,
Yet you will just know,
Once you arrive.

The grief that bleeds from your heart
Is the love not reciprocated,
it was a trap set for you,
who is simply meant to seek God.

The storm will engulf you,
Possibly for lifetimes,
Until He clears the dust for you,
When you want to seek answers.

When you don't obsess to seek,
When you become still,
The answers will come to you,
Maybe like the rainbow amidst the clouds.

You will break into a smile,
Amidst the tears,
Which will be very beautiful,
As there was a huge realisation in it.

You will cry like a baby,
Relentlessly to seek God,
Just as you cried
Being separated from your mother.

The moment will be so sacred to you,
But you need to be distanced from the crap,
You have been surrounding yourself with,
Especially your own narrative.

You may not believe,
But things will unfold for you,
One by one, so that you
absorb the soul shock gracefully.

Like the mother that loves her new born,
His love will embrace you tightly,
He being the biggest creator
Also the destroyer of your mind games.

You will reach a place
Where nothing more makes sense,
Or gives you a sense of calm,
Until you realise your own truth.

The reason for strife,
The whys and hows lead you to Him,
The traps laid by the devil,
To not follow your path to God.

You wouldn't have to defend,
or fight for your 3D connections,
Because now you simply arrived at truth,
With profound realisations.

You will cry relentlessly,
because of the sheer love,
You will feel for Him and
his unconditional ways

You will arrive and how,
Yet the path will be unfolded to you,
Based on your soul callings,
The only GPS you will need to follow.

You will be blessed,
For the pain to be taken away from you,
In the flash of a moment,
With which you struggled for so long.

This will be new you,
Your rebirth will call you
To preserve your sanity,
All will be discerned by the Spirit itself.

You will rise above the 3D,
The failing structures of which,
Won't make much difference to you,
Because now you simply know God.

Your inner child would play,
and break into a jig joyfully,
Experiencing the truth of lifetime,
Integrating itself into your adult self.

The only work that remains
Would be to do the work it takes,
After the profound realisations,
To prepare your body and mind.

To walk on the path
Then you will know
you have arrived,
With only the truth setting you free!

The Home That Speaks Love and Peace to Me

I arrived in confusion
With guilt compounded in my heart,
The pain of leaving behind my identity
To swim in the unchartered territory.

The home gave me a puzzled look
I didn't have any attachment to it either
It was just a makeshift arrangement,
I felt though for some time.

My brain keeping me awake at night,
With twirls back and forth,
The new place tried to absorb my presence
Although compulsively.

Yet I gathered strength to make it my own,
After two days of living in a limbo,
I woke up with determination,
to clean up the space.

The home attuned to my energies,
It calmed me down,
just as I filled its void,
The home embraced me completely.

With not much ado,
Just calm and poise,
Just as I treated it with
love and care.

It welcomed me alike a doting mother,
It gifted me with a safe sanctuary,
Soaking me with light and peace,
Like the morning glory of the Sun.

I dusted each of its corners
Just like I cleansed myself of all the fears
Of leaving all the negativity behind,
To start anew like a clean state.

The home loved watching me sing and dance,
Being happy and occupying space
Which was claimed by none until now,
Both became long lost friends.

Just when I began to meditate
It soothed my nerves with its poise,
When I sat to read the scriptures,
It gifted me with so much ease.

It embraced me with
the cool comforting winds,
The home was happy, because it had someone,
Who looks after it dearly.

Whatever I wanted, it gifted me
With love and belongingness,
Even when I stepped out for errands
It was eager to see me coming back.

I calmed its anxiety of being left unattended,
Just as it calmed mine, simply being in solitude.
Like a book I was never inclined to read,
It kept me embossed in its magical spell.

The home was simply happy to serve me
After a long time,
As if it had manifested my existence
Just like me manifesting peace after ages.

I knew I had simply arrived
To a space which I call it 'My home',
This home speaks to me of love,
peace and belongingness ☺

The Pregnant Pause

What is not important is
Whether you take a pause or not,
But how quickly you arrive at it,
By simply allowing it to take space.

How life has shaped up for you?
In all the phases for you?
How steadily the work flowed?
In the slow sunny afternoons at the office.

You were simply not at home,
That pause was building currency for you,
It talked many things of work,
solidarity and friendships.

The days when you were at school?
There was a pause felt at your home,
Your home missed you,
while you were replete with fun.

The time when you were expecting?
How did the waiting serve you?
To hold your bundle of joy in your arms,
Patiently waiting for it with a heavy pause!

Each pause you intend to take
Should be welcomed with being open to it,
Why are you afraid of the pause now?
Just because you are too old for it?

No, the reason is you still don't believe
In the time when it calls for it,
You have this fear of missing out,
But can you believe it to be precious?

You may have worked in corporates
You may have had fun times in University
You may have worked for your kids,
But have you have worked for you?

The constant churning with the clock,
With lunches to be packed
With no time to drape yourself
in your favourite maroon saree?

You quickly dressed up for work,
Without the need to collecting yourself
That seated within you is a divine feminine,
Who desires to be cherished for who she is.

The need of the hour is not more activity
But more pauses to retrieve your soul
From the time-woven web of tasks
Which innately makes you to forget your soul.

Hence, when life desires to gift you with a pause
Welcome it wholeheartedly
Don't be sceptical or deny its importance,
It is here for a reason – To make you smile again ☺

Illusion v/s Reality

When the mind affirms certainties
You wonder if it is your pattern,
However you strive
to not to bypass it as a snow-flake.

You try to protect
The connection fiercely
only to find it slipping
Alike sand from your closed fists.

The intensity of the connection
Beckon you to express your truth,
It gladdens you because
you found your muse.

But as the leaves begin
to shred in their seasonal glory,
The garden turns pale,
Signalling the end of the season.

You realise it coming,
yet scream it's not over yet,
Yet another time,
The sting ruminates until you heal.

You arrive at your senses,
To calm yourself from the chaos,
The PTSD that worked up your brain,
Only to take cognizance of the reality.

You claim your distance from the drama
until it's time to take charge
The mind plays a tug of war
with your heart.

Yet the heart simply knows,
It comes into acceptance sooner,
It grieves in the space,
With no-one to judge you.

The space heals you with its solitude,
this is the best retreat for your soul
To retrieve from the loss of a dream,
Which may never come true.

Time heals the trauma,
until it feels insignificant,
The soul devours the new found peace,
More than seeking to be loved.

You lean inward to find,
Seated within you is a father wound
That has never allowed you to trust men,
The wound is staring point blank at you.

You pay gratitude to your higher self,
For recognising your real wounds
Than keep you dangling in illusion,
You pray for the wound to heal.

The illusion had its say over you,
To make you forget you,
To not wholly serve you
if you escape your responsibility.

You understand what needs to be healed
Your mind more than your heart,
Devoid of being irresponsible,
Healing your inner- child within!

The narrative that plays on loop
Comes to a periodic halt,
to make your soul heard,
and listen to what it has to say.

Your soul awakens yet another time,
To retrieve its senses and pray to God,
For God speed healing,
with reality reigning heavy over anything else.

Yet you begin to bleed in surrender
And try to accept whatever is present,
Because you now know that your soul
Simply chooses its truth!

You begin your journey,
To simply start living as ordinary,
Without inflating your spiritual ego,
as a beloved child of God!

You transcend the tests given by Him,,
Only to begin the process of ascension,
To see beyond the illusions,
To be embodied with His Divinity itself! Amen! So it is.

The Pedestal

When you don't realise your true self
You will seek something,
To make you feel heard,
An external force that does the work for you.

You drown yourself in low self-esteem
because you are dependent
on how others feel about you,
You downsize your potential.

You play an underdog,
Inspite of being bestowed with unique talents
which make you a distinct personality
You wait for others to clap for you.

You scream, to make yourself heard
Yet there is no one who gets you,
Though you meet someone who does it all for you,
Only to put them on a pedestal.

Their façade impresses you,
Embosses you to your worth,
You feel happy to finally acknowledge
That someone values you, as you are.

The pedestal goes higher
You begin to worship them
Without doubting that they may be doing it
For reasons best known to them.

You nudge irrelevant thoughts
Seek validation from the person
until they feel famished
To continue doing it relentlessly for you.

You suddenly realise something is amiss,
But you nudge it saying everything is fine,
Only to realise the pedestal was a façade
To have a hold on your mind.

They played you with dark empathy,
A game of manipulation
Making you stick to their charm
To weave you in grief.

Suddenly you find the pedestal is empty
The person who validated you has disappeared
your happiness remains hard to retrieve,
You let your emotions take over your reasoning.

You cry being disappointed
Because you made them the source of validation,
Your ego is shattered by the inner voice,
Which likes to take charge of the empty pedestal.

You panic- how this could happen
How could someone disappoint you?
After all they were meant to stay,
Was a belief you try to assimilate in your heart.

You collect the broken pieces,
To weave them intricately,
This time not for anybody else,
You begin to validate yourself.

You feel overwhelmed with the loss
Yet try to build your own worth
By picking yourself up
Never to rely on anybody else.

You become your own pedestal,
You begin to realise that you are worthy
Despite the world not acknowledging you,
You are beautiful as you are.

Your soul begins to shine again,
You own your brilliance to realise.
That you are a shining star of the constellation,
That needs no pedestal to determine your worth!

A Soul Shock Towards Ascension

When nothing goes right,
You believe one more time,
In a time bound narrative,
To seek a leftover breadcrumb from them.

You keep believing in the illusion
That love is meant to find you someday
To be your happily ever after,
A belief-- that overshadows your storms.

You are caught in the eye of it,
because it strangles you,
More into its complexities
Only to famish you of your energies.

You meet another soul
Who has been through the same trauma,
Only to find some respite
From the ongoing battles.

You feel safe in their proximity
That leaves an impact on you as if,
They are meant to be your permanent escape,
Because you make them your sojourn.

Their presence feels like home,
But it simply resembles
your dysfunctional patterns of childhood,
Yet you're immature to deal with the illusion.

Your soul thrives in their camaraderie,
Only to keep you glued
But you don't realise that
they filled a void within you.

Time happens in its weird ways,
Only to reveal their real face,
They trigger open the can of worms
Bringing your past wounds to surface.

You simply feel betrayed
To ask God, "Why me?",
But He gives you time
to seek all your answers,

Not to hurt you,
But to realise your ultimate truth
That your calling is Higher
Than any other beings on the planet.

You are His Chosen One,
And whenever his Child will falter
He will bring on a mending stick,
To bring you back to your own truth.

He will make you realise that you are
Not meant for love in the 3D realm,
Love was only meant to be a lesson for you,
Because He doesn't want you to lose more time.

You chasing more irrelevant things
And people who won't serve you,
He knows your calling is higher,
Hence the soul shock that comes to you.

You feel that the punishment is gruellest
Because it came with a soul connection,
You come into radical acceptance
Until you completely transform yourself.

You will still experience
The synchronicities in place,
But you know the pain won't subside
Until your soul heals to ascend.

This lesson came to you
As the cumulative pain you experienced
From life and people in the past
Only to turn towards God.

In how many more ways will you
Betray your soul purpose?
That you keep triangulating it,
With your physical desires of the 3D?

When would you take the call?
To stay away from the worldly influences
That make you a sponge,
leading you to darkness you don't deserve?

The soul allows you to grieve
But it expects you to wake up,
And follow your North
without being distracted.

You learn to settle your nerves
And take stock of what is,
Instead of judging others,
Because it was never about them.

It was always about you,
The Soul shock was sent to you on purpose,
As a final call to arrive at the destination,
As His Chosen one and follow His word

To be a beacon of Love and Light
To forgive others unconditionally
To use your spiritual gifts,
and help humanity towards Ascension!

The Daily Practice

Sometimes you have to,
keep coming back to yourself
With nothing to look forward to
Except your will power.

You begin with the daily practise
Of forgiving your heart
For what you have put it through
Because you were naïve.

You visit His Sacred Sanctuary—his abode
To seek blessings for your heart
You continue to believe whatever transpired
Was a lesson to bring you closer to God.

You feel liberated as if some baggage
Is taken off from your soul
Your soul begins to feel lighter
As you light a lamp and offer flowers to God.

Your body feels the need to shed
The layers of pain
By simply dancing at your own pace
Which is in sync with your heart.

Your soul simply knows that
Your body needs expression
Hence it allows you to swing
The twirls unload most of your heavy emotions.

And there emerges a smile from within
Which reflects itself in your eyes
Just alike a rainbow
Amidst the dark clouds in ether.

You dance in sync with your soul
Your heart healing itself
The ecstasy is watched over by God,
Yet he knows His Child will heal soon.

Your breathe feels heavy as it purges
A lot of emotions as you dance
Hence you calm your breathe
Which calms your mind in sync too.

The soul silently chants
The name of God with each breathe
The purging is felt within
Wherein your breathe slows down.

The toxicity is annihilated by the sweat
You wash away the blues with cold water
Only to feel rejuvenated in your body
Which is a safe sanctuary to you.

You begin to trust your body
Than your emotions and feelings
And remove yourself from any situation
That feels intrusive to your body.

You nourish your body with food,
You have always enjoyed to cook,
With peace reigning in your heart
And a promise to look after your health everyday.

You close the day with a prayer
Asking God and angels to protect you
From negative entities
That are detrimental for your well-being.

You realise you are special to God
Because He wouldn't have
Interfered in your free-will
claiming whatever you thought was right.

You wait for Him to show the path
To be fearless to claim His grace
To be aware of the obstacles
To surpass them with your discernment.

Only to find Him waiting for you to arrive
At the other end of the tunnel
With infinite love, for you,
With you becoming your Highest version! So it is!

Life Through a New Lens

When love feels like an illusion
You seldom understand
It was a dysfunctional trait.
That played its term.

You kept seeking love in wrong places
Where it was never meant to be
Because you never saw the patterns
Running through veins, alike blood.

You accepted defeat
And kept coming back to yourself
Hurt, by people you came across
Who never deserved your energies.

It was time that played games with you
you couldn't understand why it went wrong
Inspite of you being good enough,
Though you blamed yourself.

Time did not make you stronger
It was the health and its damage thereof,
That wore the repercussions
of your past wounds.

You muster the courage to examine
The bare wounds
That still ooze the pain of unrequited
love from your caretakers

Inspite of being gifted so profoundly
By the Divine himself
You ask for forgiveness
for the injustice you did to your soul.

You learn the lessons
That unfold one by one,
You give it time and patience
Because you betrayed your heart

To take all the crap
Without taking a stand for yourself
Do you even remember when
did you smile with all your heart?

It is now time to integrate your heart
And make it whole again
To forgive yourself for the wrongs
You did unto itself.

It is now time to heal your soul
To come into balance and
To love yourself unconditionally,
Others were incapacitated to do for you.

It is time to put on another lens
To see what transpired
And also heal your generational trauma,
in the action you have been avoiding.

It is time to rise and shine
To see what the truth is
To defend your heart and soul
From the dis-eased part of you.

It is time to be a new you
A complete, human,
Who knows to cherish her femininity
And also, to balance her masculinity.

There is mercy in His kingdom
When it's your time to receive,
you don't know the huge blessings,
He is about to shower upon you.

It is a wake-up call for you Starseeds!
For the formation of New Earth,
To raise the vibrations of the prisoner planet
And assist humanity in acknowledging the Ultimate Truth!

Depths of Love

How often have you felt loved?
What is the real meaning of love?,
Is it the mere infatuation
That holds the keys to your heart.

Is it the bitter truth?
love is but a sweet nectar
That brushes you off,
without your cognizance.

It is the tug you feel in your heart,
When a friend understands your silence,
It is the venom when it roasts a genuine friendship
But have you ever experienced the depths of love?

A love so profound that surpasses all notions
All beliefs, and traditions known,
It exists in the all-pervading
essence of the spirit.

The rhythmic beating of your heart,
The offering of flowers to God,
The laughter of a child,
The deep gaze of a lover into your eyes,

Are the depths of love, one can find.
The holding of hands,
The forgetting of self in meditation
is love you cannot behold within.

The depths of love is in inclusion
In deep forging of bonds with the other,
A perfect semblance of
care and understanding

The depths of the love, is your mind
Radiating love and light,
in transcendence that holds the key,
To the spirals of your heart.

It is forgiveness,
It is not defining who others should be
But being responsible for your kindness,
In this mad, cruel world.

The depths of love, is
being love to every soul you meet,
And respect their journey,
Devoid being judgemental about their choices.

It is understanding others,
Devoid the need to be controlled,
The depths of love, is
humble union with your higher self.

It is the game of total surrender,
Which is the undermined lesson of life,
It is coming to a realisation that,
Love is the answer to every situation of Life!

A Shift in Perspective

When it's your calling,
When it is your time,
You will simply know,
Because you will be His Chosen one.

You would try to do things
In the same ways you did in the past
Yet you will feel a growing urge
To outgrow the patterns of the past

You will look around
You will lose things dear to you,
A job, a friendship or a city you stayed for long,
Which never served you or your soul.

It was the ego that operated
On your behalf, binding you
To be on this roller coaster
journey of emotions.

The tower moment arrives in any form,
A failed dream, a loss, an ailment,
But you wonder what went wrong
Because you did everything on your part.

You will realise that you have been hit
By a gazillion bricks on your mind,
The games the ego has played onto you
Making you a collateral damage in time.

There is profound darkness to deal with
Just like the moon derives its light from the Sun,
You cannot trace your shadows
Because the night is never ending.

You try to keep up your spirit
However in an isolated moment
The veil drops unguarded,
letting out a profuse cry.

You allow the tears to flow,
You cry your heart out, since
There is no one to judge you
You become your own judge

The ego apologizes profoundly to God
And surrenders its control of your life,
It knows how nasty it has been
In ruining your peace and health over years.

Your soul consoles you,
It embraces you tightly like a mother
Yet forgives you for what cannot be undone,
You arrive at a place, where the last tear drops.

The storm clears itself after some time,
The Sun shines again when you feel God
In your soul, loving you unconditionally,
Because he has been waiting for you to return.

You realise how much you have sabotaged
the connection you always had with Him
He holds you once again
On your path, only meant for you.

Your soul has a new perspective
It guides you
with each little step you take,
Towards a new beginning, a new you!

Soham

It dawns upon you sooner or later
that you are one of the selected few
To be a part of the soul healing program
Amidst the greeneries that gladdens you.

You arrive at a place known to you
Though it makes you see things differently
with a new perspective,
Making you a seeker.

You get acquainted to the daily schedule
Which feels rigid to the old you,
Because you have never witnessed
The soothing calm prior to the dawn.

You manage your time
Tripping a little bit,
you do the Shuddhi-kriyas
To cleanse the blockages in your body.

Your body adapts itself
slowly to the new routine,
The Netis know you well than your body,
You need to absolve your fears.

Time warms up in the cosy temple
Where mind and body integrate with the soul
The temple perfectly named as 'Manan',
which crafts the rest of your journey.

The asana practices begin
to relax the body and mind,
With 'Shavasan'
stealing the glory of all other asanas

As the body graduates with
its own movements
The breathe follows que
at a rhythmic pace,

Installing a sense of calm and
serenity to the mind
Which integrates beautifully as
a mind-body-soul dynamic.

The rigidity within loosens
To have clarity of mind,
followed with the breath work,
The system encapsulates itself with ease.

As the pranayama session concludes
It paves way to yet another session
Of Chanting the vibrant Bhramari,
The master game changer of mental health.

Every chant of Om and Nn feels
like an offering to God
Your inner world inundates itself
with profound ecstasy and joy

The reverberations of which
you feel in your soul
Which let you know you
have simple arrived.

The session ends with a
chirpy calm in your heart
The Om Stavana proclaims its glory
to the rising kundalini

You begin to realise'I am that'
which simply is the soul of SOHAM,
You realise that there is no one stopping you
Than your own mind.

You have gratitude for everything,
You explored in your program,
You feel like there is this magic seed
embedded within you.

The light will never fail you,
If you show up on the path consistently,,
Which is the beautiful culmination of the program
Yet a beginning, a rebirth of a New You!

Many Lives Many Masters

To be born in a human body
Is a gift from the Divine,
A sacred journey which unfolds
The lessons in each lifetime.

The reincarnation is the next step
towards soul evolution,
However it presents itself
as an ending, in the 3D.

The soul is born again
Yet is capacitated to forget
its previous roles
its past lives as a human,

We chose our mother
And the family we are born into,
Before incarnation, along with the people
Who we meet in this lifetime.

The soul graduates itself over lifetimes,
Goes through the experiences
A path which it follows
As per its soul contract.

The people who we find most
difficult to deal with
Are placed for our soul to grow
To graduate with a lesson meant for us.

So don't hate the experiences
you go through
Instead grow through them
To progress towards soul liberation.

Forgive them, and thank them
For a role they played in your life
they served you as your anchor
For healing your soul.

Your journey will be blessed
If you forgive others unconditionally
And learn to let go of
what doesn't serve you

You will learn as a soul
To shed all the layers of your ego
And begin to operate from soul
With happiness emerging from the Source.

You will lose everything dear to your ego
The fears, anxieties and the phobias
That gripped you for long time-
when you learn the soul lesson.

Your soul will feel liberated
You will arrive
In all glory,
with endless stream of bliss and joy,

When it is time for you to ascend
To higher dimension,
You will simply know,
To follow His Divine Light.

The soul will thrive with Love
Even in between the lifetimes,
The only grace would be His Light
Encompassing every inch of your soul!

To merge in His infinite Love and light
Would be the goal of each lifetime
With you as a soul born in a human body
And to experience life in its fullest expression of Love!

Galaxies and Their Pathways

The space between our worlds
Is alike a never ending black-hole

We collide,
We drift.

We return to our orbits.
Where space is oblivious to the happenings

Sometimes I wonder
What it is to be a free electron

It doesn't know its origin
But it does feel belonged to the space

It doesn't intend to claim,
This is the reason it stands unwavering

The stardust is replete with chaos
Yet is afraid to admit

which remains subtly undefined
The light years can't take away what we have between us

For now time keeps us in sync
Maybe the apprehension is you know it evidently too

The rigidity of our galaxies,
Is that they no longer shimmer nor emote,

Because, the space between our worlds is alike
The forever expanding blackhole.

Loveful Chaos

A hug, an embrace,
A dormant feeling she cannot bypass
Evading a whirlpool of storms
Beneath her skin.

It consumes her, like wildfire
Engulfing her being.
Until it becomes her
Until it breathes life through her.

Waning off the righteousness
Scaling up the narratives on love
A periodic dance,
A loop on re-runs.

Beginning to embrace her
in its entirety,
Until it scares her of its
magnanimous presence.

Souls colliding in the erratic trance
Of a star studded night
Candles and soft music,
Making her feel at ease.

The ether pulls a blanket to hide itself
While the dark pours relentlessly
Witnessing the melting of their bodies,
Too close to merge inside the other.

Their eyes glide and melt
In the possibility of a loving communion
A guarded warrior pulls her guards down
Only to be showered with love.

Spoiling every grain of her skin
The soul breathes heavy
In the close proximity of love
Coyness steers out of her way

Enabling her to submit herself.
Into his embrace
Huge enough to hold her vulnerabilities
in his space.

She smiles coyly
Closing her eyes
Submerging in the shower of his love
Her cup overflowing in the same way.

She trembles
As he touches her soul
He loves her the way she desires
Spoiling her from head to toe.

She moans in a way that pleases him
She wants more as she submits more
He thrusts his way inside her
To explore darker truths about her.

Transforming her pain into Love
She smiles through her tears
The night recedes at its own pace,
As they envelop in each other's arms.

He sleeps sound after a long time,
She stays awake adoring his loving presence
And the mystery of the magical night
The dawn arrives coyly

As she begins to fall asleep
She hides behind the sheets
To sleep peacefully,
Calming her chaos.

Until peace becomes
her second skin
And breathes love into
her soul anew.

Touch

A hug, an embrace.
Or simply holding hands

The merging of finite energetic fields
Between you and me

The entwining of our hearts
A memory dancing on the re-runs.

Breathing in vacuum waiting
To be revisited.

To be cherished.
To be recreated

In the halls of my forlorn cynical breaths
That fetches your image as a default

Burning in the desires
Of the acquainted past

The images wear shades of grey
On the landscape of my heart

Which has now become redundant
It flows of vacuum with memories that linger.

I wish a day comes when I forget
About what touch feels like or

Become numb to fathom
The rhythmic patterns of

My forever throbbing heart
That churns memories in agony

I wish the pain is no longer mine to carry
But for the earth to ground it.

For the skies to dissolve it in space
For the words to carry in poems

For the seas to drown the voice
For the ingrained memory casket

For time that wouldn't remain the same
untouched with the touch I no longer claim.

Deep Incisions

If you cut
Sew me back

Weave tapestries with love
as the wound oozes viscously

Entangle with the mess
Because, only you can

I cannot hold for too long
That which no longer claims to be me.

The dark and cold
Has made me frozen.

Let's see if you have the courage
To see me melt again

Don't question, just witness
If you only have the heart

To watch me burn
Don't be afraid– to be washed away

The ocean runs deep,
However the tides will

throw you back –like crap,
From a place –if you don't belong.

Unrequited Love

The constant yearning
To be in communion with the other,
To seek a response or two?

Is nothing but to beg for
what doesn't exist in totality.
These projections

are the unhealed aspects of your being,
The core wounds and shadows are
The patterns of engaging with the world.

Is it just an illusion,
You assume to be true?
There isn't anything called unrequited love.

The love you never offered to yourself,
Comes a full circle and the people you meet
Mirror the same deficit onto you.

You create barriers, for no-one to enter
The viel is hard enough to trespass
around your metallic guarded soul.

You blame people for not loving you enough,
When you did not offer it
generously to yourself.

There's nothing called unrequited love
There are wounds that need light,
There are patterns to break.

There is no blame game
There is no black sheep
There's an ocean of love–

for you waiting endlessly.
For you to come awake
For you to meet you, where you are.

Not where you are supposed to be,
When you even catch a glimpse of this ocean,
You would nevertheless flow like a river towards it.

You will start letting go
Like the river does—
You will start letting it all in.

When you receive and willing to seek
Let this receiving begin with you
Because there's nothing called unrequited love

The closed doors, reroutes and cliff-hangers
Are the only the signs you need to take a U turn from.

Rest

Sleep is rest for the body,
Silence is rest from constant communication.

Stillness is rest from constant activity
Withdrawal is rest from preoccupation.

Exercise is rest from lethargy,
Poetry is rest from the common prose.

Music is rest from the linear lyrics,
Meditation is rest from the relentless chatter.

Anything that relaxes you more than the preceded action
is rest.
How have you been resting today?

Love Expressions

The light that pierces through the dark voluminous night
Is the love that radiates into the ether.

The wind-chime swirling with the breeze
Is an expression of appreciation for the other.

The gibberish talks of an infant with his mother–
In an attempt to seek her attention.

To respond is to express
a holy communion between the souls.

Between what is said and unsaid
To communicate is to establish a connection.

And all the forms are the expressions of love
Poetry, songs, music, dance or art forms.

We know love
But we refrain to express it much

A child is an expression of love for the mother
Creation is an expression of love by the Creator.

Music is an expression of love for the lyrics
Dance an expression of ecstasy a body cannot hold.

What is your expression of love?
How would you respond when love finds you?

Would you feel intimidated or would be open to receive?
Have you made your-self as an expression of love

Love as in its purest form
Devoid attachment and obsessions.

Can you love freely?
Can you still express your love for the other without owning them?

Is something you need to ponder upon,
Is your life an expression of love?

Are you as a life an expression of love?
These questions hold the deepest vision and the prime keys to evolve.

Void

I see you,
I feel you

I hear you
I acknowledge you.

You have something to say
You repress from the toxicity of the world

When the noise gets louder
Old soul- there's nothing that catches

Your attention for long,
The authenticity you crave for is a cliched word.

The pompous, insincere, world
Cannot give you what you seek.

Hence you retrench into a cocoon-
a dark fearful place for many.

The pain of being birthed again
is enormous.

The bottomless pit spirals further
into nothingness.

I know you're busy
You have to travel great lengths

To connect with the outside world,
When the fragile coñnection is not established.

Your pain gets louder,
Screams of the futility of its efforts

Leave this drama,
You have played this enough.

Now it's time to heal and be at your own pace
Do not look outside dear void,

There's no one outside to take care of you,
Seek within before without

The treasures are calling you,

To embrace you with love abundance happiness and prosperity

Your soul has ever imagined in all lifetimes,

Trust in receiving and believe what you seek is seeking you too.

Transition

The voice absolves deep into the void,
Yet another time.

Love visits,
Barging through her armour precariously.

For not too long as a visitor,
Its playfulness makes her grin wider

Reinstating long lost charms,
Forcibly rendering her out of her cocoon,

For the first time the outside feels warm too
her armour falls inadvertently,

Devoid her cognizance,
Only to make way for the thorns to prick.

Whilst the dreamy aroma still engulfs her being,
The gripping claws make their presence

Loud and clear,
Until she stops listening to the music

The wind chimes drop their playfulness,
Making way for the warning bells.

Only to succumb to the ever increasing disparity,
With what still remains a delusion.

The cocoon waves at her again,
But she doesn't fit in anylonger.

For all the time she was outside,
Her wings appear unknowingly.

She makes them flutter with a noise,
Until she believes she can fly.

The cocoon waves her goodbye,
Teary eyed, because it knows

The transition would be a challenging period for her,
The fiery light blurs her vision for now,

Being soaked in darkness for long,
But her wings make way for her to fly,

To embrace all the abundance,
Life has yet to offer.

Love Letter to My Body

Hello, my beautiful body!
It's been a long time,
I have ever acknowledged you,
For the vital role you played in my life,

I am so grateful to you, I wish,
I could have been more thankful to you,
in my formative years
You have managed an entire Universe within me.

You have been my daily vessel,
To perform my duties, tasks and roles
Fluently and effortlessly for years,
With no complaints.

I thank you, for serving me so well
I love my heart that keeps throbbing every day,
Like a unsaid promise,
Meet people and gain experiences for my soul.

I thank you my brain,
For absorbing and understanding,
Life, love and losses in same stride,
Without being cynical about it for too long.

I love my legs who have taken me places,
Walks and trails and
even hiking at places
You have carried me well.

I love my eyes,
Deep like an ocean and unpredictable
They hold so much mysteries and pain,
Yet brighten up with smallest things of life.

I love my lips,
They have sealed and concealed
Many dark truths about people
Yet remaint defiant while dealing with injustice.

I love you, my womb
Who has been a vessel, to carry and protect,
And nurture a magic called life within me,
Honouring me to become a mother.

I love my curls, my crowning glory for years,
I have loved their bounce and shine.
The greys now depict the wisdom of years passed by,
I promise to take care of you.

I love my hands that enabled me to
Work, create and hold my bundle of joy
In my arms, when my child was still a baby,
To hug a loved one with deep love and reverence.

I am grateful for my stomach
That keeps on churning food and providing
Strength to my heart, body and mind,
At all the times.

I am grateful for my ears and nose,
For functioning everyday,
From listening to soft music and mantras
And smelling aromas to smelling something fishy.

I am grateful to you my body
For being a vessel for me on this planet
Through which I, perform everyday
The most simple and difficult tasks in equanimity.

It has been a beautiful journey for decades
And it will be for the rest of the lifetime.
I promise to take care of you,
With nourishing foods and actions good for you.

I can't thank-you enough for serving me so well
I will ensure you are treated best every day,
Let us forge a beautiful journey ahead with love,
To enable us to live a bigger, brighter future for both of us!

There Is Only One You

Have you ever wondered, what makes you, You?
Your values, beliefs and dreams are an integral part of you.

Being fearless in the pursuit of the dreams that keep you awake,
The core essence of your being that forges a path ahead for you.

Be ready and be in the now, to never miss an opportunity
Because it can pass you by, if you are not attentive.

Work more harder, doesn't matter if you fail
Cry yourself out, but then dust yourself and move on.

In the pursuit of the new goals awaiting you
For you to rise like a phoenix.

Make your own choices and act on them
Because only they can define your worth in the long run.

Stand in your own truth fearlessly
Knowing that you won't be appreciated always,

Don't try to fit in, because you were never meant to,
Be proud of how you sailed through everything.

Be nothing but you, because Life is awaiting,
For you to arrive fearless, fierce and flawed.

What Makes You Special?

When you know you are different
Than most of the people you meet,
You make an effort to fit in,
For you to feel belonged.

The absurdity of the trail and error
To really fit in the shoes of the other
Is an uphill task, which makes you feel
As if you are an outsider on the planet.

But after some point in time, you realise
It is futile fitting yourself in
Or being acknowledged as regular
When you understand that you might be special.

In the norm of being accepted by all
You seldom fail to shine bright or worst
Even own your own light,
Which in all sacredness is not the right thing.

You examine, you observe closely
How am I different from the rest?
What are the innate abilities I am gifted with?
That makes me really special.

How do I really honour my uniqueness?
Than devoting myself to be accepted by the other,
Becomes a compelling quest for you to determine
Your worth and uniqueness devoid the ego game.

To be accepted by the other needs work
Because being different stands predominantly alone
Mocked, booed, shied away from the crowd
But we prefer working hard to be seen.

But the humility and preciousness is in
Evolving with your unique traits,
Which is your greatest blessing,
Than claiming to be whom you are not!

What Does Fun Mean to Me?

Fun to me is being me
Forgetting my adult self
And being child like
Simply being me devoid veils.

Fun to me is a game of table-tennis
Tossing the ball from one end to the other
Never missing the shot, infact
Giving a sweep backhand to the opponent.

Fun to me is the laughter and chaos the game brings
With chase and attention scaling,
Close encounters with the bat and the ball,
Trying to notch the tables, from One-Love to Game!

Fun to me is wearing Tees and shorts
And scaling up the small mountains on a rainy day
Weathering the fog and the drizzles
To watch a distant rainbow in the light.

Fun for me is canvas and colours
From sketching a rough zentangle to
A fully coloured doodle art or boho art wall painting,
From black pen to colour bombing the scape.

Fun for me is being child-like
Simply watching the star lit sky endlessly
To speak my heart out with a friend
Listening to and singing songs with delight!

Fun for me is dancing in my room alone,
Or better dancing with my friends
To the beats of the unsung songs that
Fill my cup of smiles and laughter with glee!

Fun for me is watching my child grow
And make noodles and tea for me,
The astonished mother in me feels proud
Of the kid that mothers her some-times!

Fun for me is singing songs and hymns
In the praise of the Divine,
A relentless offering my heart offers Him
Every single day of my existence.

Fun for me is me waking up
Without alarms for the next day
Yet knowing what needs to be done,
For the day to work out smoothly.

Fun for me is being child like
And sleeping on my mothers lap
Being caressed by her love,
Forgetting all the stressors for a while.

Fun for me is being me
Simply enjoying being me
Without judgements or being called names
The grown-ups usually do!

Fun for me is being in the moment
Simply dissolving myself into it
Being one with it,
Breathing life into my rigid old self!

Let Me

Let me love you the way I want to
Let me touch your soul

Let me hold you
to feel your presence

Let me hear what your silence
has yet not conveyed

Let me be loved the way my soul wants to
Let me listen to your heartbeat

Let me understand your silence
So that I can understand mine

Let me be mine before I can be yours
Let me be for a while before you leave

Let me feel silence exudes
more love than words do

Let me know that these colours
are for next lifetime

Let me be whole without
being broken

Let me look at the universe and
proclaim how you complete me

Let me stay before
you loosen your embrace

Let me seek refuge in your warmth
enough to last a season

Let me go, coz I am afraid my tears
will meet you again

Let me be the one whom
your heart cherishes forever.

Gifted

Gifted we are in so many ways
A special feeling that brightens our days.

A skill that envelopes our being
An honour that makes us feel seen,

A blessed feeling that brings us to life
In all bleak moments we learn to survive

To honour the calling we have within
Destined moments that unfold seeking

Treasures that are deep uncovered
To make the gifted being discovered.

The Gift of Life

What a precious gift it is
To wake up in the morning

To breathe fresh air,
And see the light of the new day.

To make plans and work through the day
With grit and determination in our ways.

To see the world with our beautiful eyes
To respond in ways with a steady smile,

To walk with our feet firm on the ground
To dabble with ideas that seem profound

To work everyday to fulfil our dreams
Until life feels like a beautiful stream

With joy and success adorning our way
And happiness making a beautiful stay.

How precious it is to be gifted with life,
The only gift we learn to respect,

In all odds and situations restored,
To honour Him and his precious gift bestowed.

Finding Happiness in Everyday Life

The birds chirping at dawn
The sunrise across the window
The coffee brewing its aroma around
The peace of the morning that surrounds.

The cool breeze on a warm day
The fragrance of fresh flowers
Light music that paves its way
For a musical start of the day.

The story that weaves its way
Through the mystical pages of the novel
A canvas enchanted with colours
On an Uninterrupted slow afternoon

A slow evening that winds up the day
With your favourite cuppa
Is the taste of a good life
With a magical touch of happiness.

Closure

She is picking up the broken pieces
a closure compounds with clarity.

It was the last sting
Now everything depends on her

To move ahead and heal in peace
Despite everything that has happened.

For the masculine to face his dreadful truth
For the feminine to reclaim her power

The last straw to dismantle the
Enmeshed toxicity between them.

The Feminine is hurt and wounded
Over things she never did

The masculine is overwhelmed
Because he was mirrored his weaknesses

Their individual truths hurt them silently
She prefers to heal in silence more than ever.

Acknowledging and accepting to love her
Shadows and light with equanimity.

A distressful calm before she takes off
Brilliantly and brightly again.

With a promise to reclaim her essence
Godspeed, along with self-love and light.

Muse

You triggered within her
Something that died eons ago

She was proud of the tough barriers
That never ever melted

Inspite of the scorching Sun,
Now, how will she console her brave little heart

That all it endured was not for real
The price she paid for being alive again

Was the muse you gifted to a
Star studded fighter?

Vent

And after a while,

It rumbles like a huge scream
Blowing up storms in your psyche

The image they built brick by brick
Was a gimmick to rusticate your soul

To enslave you in ways you couldn't comprehend
Nor could they be guilty of deceiving.

Your love wasn't enough to melt their heart
Where you thrived to make yourself seen

The inseparable collaboration was a place
to hold you back from your own shadow.

Restricting to show you their pseudo side
Occupying you with abnormalities and strife

They knew they lost it when you left
sans a battle unfought

Where little could be repaired
through their redundant apologies

The condescending ways traumatized
The little child within you.

The latter felt attacked in their energetic space
Their toxicity ignited the demons of the past

In a whirlwind trip of emotional chaos
A path which you dread to tread ever again.

A path which has rendered you an empty soul
when it couldn't fall for their gimmicks

The heart called back its soul
From further delusions

The war is still ON not with words
But internalising all that was left unsaid

The little child is walking his way back home
Hoping this time it won't go astray

He is tired and wants to retreat in his shell
To simply be and to go back to himself.

To retrieve the beauty and space
With peace being his only soulmate.

Art

They were wound mates
They had the same wounds

She thought it was love
His silence made it awfully flawed

Now the wound doesn't ooze
Because she prefers dressing it with art

The heart has built its fortresses overtime
Scars are the only reminder of the battles

Fought and survived
The life throbbing force

Now bleeds through her veins
And they call it such a beautiful he"art"!

What It Is to Be a Woman

When the going gets tough
She cries herself to sleep

The darkness pulls down
The barriers she clings so tight.

She pursues the role of an
Aggressive masculine

Tired of being a perfectionist
She settles for a low profile existence

Gasping to be seen and heard
To be celebrated for who she is,

A real divine Feminine

She is exhausted from feeling
Like she's always falling behind

In some invisible race against the clock
Against other women, against herself.

She doesn't remember the beginning
But she decides to stop running

She decides instead to learn
How to be who she is

And to understand that itself is
More than enough, it's extraordinary.

Life Through a New Lens: (2.0)

Life is alike a stream
You pave your way
Through pebbles and stones
Rocks and sand, alongside the flow.

You enjoy the sparkling water
Because of the Sun that shines through it,
You keep going, almost evading
The inevitable currents of the stream.

Which nevertheless gain momentum
Without a clue of sorts
it's the nature of the stream
To seek its free flow alike the wind.

You keep walking
through the shallow waters
Witnessing tiny creatures
and pebbles.

But one uncanny stone
catches your attention
You watch its lustrous shine
being amazed.

You try not to wander
in the deep currents
Because you understand
you may not be able to

Push against the whirling
forces of the stream
You gaze the stream
endlessly till the horizon.

The sand beneath your feet
The skies above your head
The sparkling water that touches your soul
The silent roar of the winds,

You watch the perfect landscape,
You begin to walk towards the shore
Not knowing enough time has elapsed
With the sceneries that held you captive for long.

You pave your way towards home
Carrying the gifts of nature in your heart
You witness something has loosened
Something has had a cleansing effect on you.

You cannot pin point to what it is,
you feel like weight lifted from your soul
There is the void which rings
in new calm into you.

You feel like you have birthed again
Like the sparkling stone that caught your attention
Your soul has a breakthrough idea
Which makes you replete with joy.

You cannot define it
You are eager to share it with everyone,
But you realise it is just a seed planted
By none other than the Divine himself.

The dark night of the soul
doesn't overwhelm you,
Because there is a magic GPS
embedded in your soul

Guiding you to take the
next baby step towards it.
You simply begin walking your path,
With a new lens in your heart

You let go of the old contracts,
Clearing the space for the unknown.

You simply to walk with faith
With a knowing that amazing things
Are Destined for you to happen,
Only if you strive to heal your soul.

You know healing is the only route
You need to take here and now
You pledge your integrity on this path
to honour yourself with everything you need.

The awakening is rude one,
it unburdens you from the guilt
Only to force awaken you how to build
From the broken findings of the past.

The ego accepts its defeat
and finally surrenders
Since it knows it can
no longer tread the path

The soul has been striving
to follow relentlessly,
Birthing a new life and
a new cycle for it to thrive!

There is no rush to claim
what you are destined to become,
Because this journey is about Love,
About You, your soul and its purpose!

An Embodiment of Love

An embodiment of love
With love as his natural state

The magic in most unusual forms
one can comprehend

Or maybe he is that which
renders an emotion a meaning.

A sanctity, a gift, a phenomenal joy
For all that have encompassed his magnetic field

All pervading, all inclusive
There are no exclusions in his aura.

A tide that rises only to accelerate
Or illuminate the path less known to you.

A steady stream of joy enveloping
The labyrinth of your soul

Decluttering and demystifying all that is
Non essential for peaceful existence.

A sound, a call from the Divine
One more time,

That makes you believe in kindness and humanity
Slowly pushing away the walls of programmed behaviour.

A breakthrough lurking to be resurfaced with
The demons in your psyche.

With the intention to dismantle the
Stringent narratives you held for eons.

An unrelenting mystery difficult to decode
However you can

Simply enjoy the very
existence of your being.

Just as you are,
Without being judged or devalued

Naked in your vulnerabilities,
Believing in the solidarity you receive.

Devoid of gamble or trickster
The armours you held for so long

Simply refuse to cling to you,
You amazingly meet your own shadow.

A love which you embodied as a child
A mirror that shines your own soul onto you.

An embodiment of love
And love being his natural state.

Emotions in Motion

One day I sat with grief
And the rivers flowed

It was nothing else but the
Pain flowing through me.

I sat with silence only to find
I wanted to write my heart out.

I sat with joy and contemplation
Only to express happiness through dance

I sat with anger only to find
The steadiness my breathe holds.

I sat with ecstasy only to understand
It is the overflowing joy within me.

One day I sat with myself
Only to understand He is always with me.

The emotions in motion is nothing but
the love your heart beholds for you.

www.ingramcontent.com/pod-product-compliance
Lightning Source LLC
La Vergne TN
LVHW041101150826
845673LV00007B/1868

* 9 7 9 8 8 9 6 3 2 7 2 4 0 *